The Forg

By Mak

The Seasons of Growing Up

The summer sun once kissed my face,
Barefoot laughter, a child's embrace.
Chasing fireflies, climbing trees,
Dreams carried high by autumn's breeze.

Then winter came, with lessons deep,
A heart once fearless learned to weep.
Spring returned, the frost grew thin,
And I found myself anew again.

Each year a chapter, turning slow,
With every storm, I learn, I grow.
Though childhood fades like melting snow,
Its echoes whisper where I go.

When We Were Young

Remember the days of scraped-up knees,
Running wild, climbing trees?
Secrets whispered in the dark,
Dreams drawn in sidewalk chalk?

The world was small but felt so wide,
No fear, no need to run and hide.
Now time has pulled us far apart,
But childhood lingers in the heart.

The Distance Between Then and Now

I used to race the wind to school,
Dirt on my hands, my pockets full—
Of pebbles, notes, and broken things,
Treasures lost in golden springs.

Now I walk, my steps more slow,
With dreams too big and fears that grow.
The world has changed, and so have I,
Yet still, I chase the endless sky.

Growing Pains

No one tells you when you're small,
That growing up means losing all—
The magic, wonder, carefree days,
Traded in for bills to pay.

Yet somewhere deep, a spark remains,
A child inside despite the chains.
For every burden, every scar,
We still wish upon a star.

Shattered Echoes

The walls still hum with your laughter,
soft echoes in an empty home.
I press my palms against the silence,
but it won't mold into your touch.

The bed still holds your shape,
a ghost of warmth where you once lay.
I sleep on the edge,
afraid of drowning in the void you left.

You are a wound that time won't stitch,
a shadow sewn into my bones.
No matter how far I run,
I carry you like a scar.

A Love Unwritten

We were a story meant for forever,
but fate held an eraser in trembling hands.
Every promise we whispered into the stars
has been smudged into nothingness.

I still trace the outlines of our could-have-beens,
pressing ink into pages torn from time.
But the ending is empty,
a sentence left unfinished.

Your name still burns in my throat,
a prayer I can't bring myself to speak.
Tell me, did I mean nothing,
or did I mean too much to be kept?

Drowning in Silence

You left without slamming the door,
no echoes, no apologies.
Just an absence so loud
it swallowed my breath.

I search for you in the spaces between words,
in the pauses of songs we used to sing.
But all I find is silence,
cold and infinite.

I whisper your name into the night,
but the darkness does not reply.
It only tightens its grip,
dragging me deeper into the void.

Hands That Let Go

You held my heart like a fragile thing,
fingertips tracing the cracks.
For a moment, I believed you'd stay,
that love was enough to keep you.

But even the softest hands can let go,
even the gentlest hearts can grow cold.
One day, you woke up
and decided I was no longer home.

I wonder if you ever felt the ache
when my name slipped from your lips.
Or if I was just another season
you were meant to leave behind.

The Ghost of You

You are the ache in my ribs,
a phantom touch lingering too long.
No matter how many times I exhale,
I still breathe you in.

The moonlight carves your outline
into my memory each night.
I close my eyes to forget,
but dreams are cruel storytellers.

I keep searching for your reflection
in places I know you'll never be.
Some ghosts don't need chains to haunt—
they only need love left unfinished.

The Art of Vanishing

There is a kind of loneliness
that makes you question if you exist.
When the phone never rings,
when your footsteps leave no trace.

You become a ghost in your own life,
haunting the spaces you used to fill.
Your reflection stares back at you,
but even the mirror refuses to remember.

People pass by, speaking with foreign tongues,
lives entwining like threads you'll never touch.
And you wonder,
if you disappeared, would the world notice?

Hollow Rooms

Alone is the sound of a door closing
with no one waiting on the other side.
It is the hum of the refrigerator at midnight,
the drip of a faucet that never stops.

It is the dust collecting on books unread,
the quiet rustle of sheets untouched.
It is hearing your heartbeat in the dark,
wondering if it beats for anyone but you.

It is the realization
that you could scream
and no one would hear.

A Room Without Windows

Loneliness is a room without windows,
no light, no voices, just time stretching on.
You learn to live with the silence,
to fill it with the sound of your own breath.

You talk to yourself,
not for answers,
but just to hear something alive.
You write letters you never send,
words dissolving into the void.

And you wonder,
if the world has forgotten you,
do you still exist?

The Weight of Air

Breathing is the one promise we keep,
a silent contract with existence.
Inhale—
the weight of the world settles in your ribs.
Exhale—
you let go of what was never yours to hold.

Some days, air is an ocean,
heavy, pressing, drowning.
Other days, it is a whisper,
light and fleeting, barely there.

Breathing is proof that we are alive,
but it does not mean we are living.

The Breath Between Words

There is a breath before goodbye,
a hesitation, a pause—
as if air could hold back the inevitable.

There is a breath before a kiss,
a moment of waiting, of knowing—
where the world narrows to a single touch.

There is a breath before a scream,
the gathering of pain, the sharp intake—
before the breaking, before the release.

Breath is the space between everything,
the quiet that shapes what we feel.

If Time Had Mercy

If time had mercy, it would bend,
And let me hold you once again.
Erase the day you slipped away,
Rewrite the dawn in a softer gray.

But time is cruel—it does not yield,
It leaves the wound but will not heal.
And so I walk this endless maze,
With only memories ablaze.

The Storm That Took You

You were the thunder before the rain,
A restless sky too full of pain.
The storm inside—too fierce, too wild,
Left us lost, left us exiled.

But even life breaks and fades,
Even darkness meets the day.
If only you had waited through,
You'd see the light that still loves you.

he House I Grew Up In

The walls still hum with laughter past,
Footsteps running, echoes cast.
A doorframe lined with pencil marks,
Proof we tried to reach the stars.

Now the halls are quiet, dim,
Memories folded, tucked within.
The house remains, yet time has flown-
I visit, but I don't belong.

The Skylines We Imagine

We build tomorrow in our sleep,
With hands too small, with hearts too deep.
Sketching futures bright and grand,
Castles rising from the sand.

Yet morning breaks, the light spills in,
Reality's hands pull us thin.
Still, we chase the sky's embrace,
Dreamers never lose their place.

What Ifs and Almosts

I walk through halls of things unsaid,
Conversations locked in thread.
What if I stayed? What if I left?
What if I tried my very best?

A thousand echoes, none reply,
Only silence asking why.
The past is done, the present near,
Yet still, I drown in what I fear.

The Broken Swing

A swing still sways where we once played,
Faded ropes, a seat decayed.
I push it gently, let it rock,
A ghost of laughter on the clock.

Time has taken what we were,
Summer nights and whispered dares.
Yet in the creak of rusted chains,
A part of us still here remains.

A Letter to My Future Self

Did you climb the tallest peak?
Did you find the things we seek?
Or did the world make you forget,
The dreams we swore to never quit?

If you are tired, rest your eyes,
But don't let go, don't compromise.
Remember me—the child who swore,
We'd always reach for something more.

We Were Here

Carved our names in wooden beams,
Swore we'd live inside our dreams.
The world was wide, the skies so tall,
We thought that we could have it all.

But time moves fast, and hands let go,
The dreams we held start melting slow.
Still, somewhere in the wind's soft hum,
The kids we were—they still run.

The Ashes Remember

The walls once hummed with love and light,
Now crumble into dust at night.
The echoes burn, the embers glow,
A home reduced to smoke and woe.

I trace the air where laughter stood,
Where warmth and safety once felt good.
But fire is cruel, it does not spare,
It swallows all, then leaves you there.

The Night We Lost Everything

The night was calm before the blaze,
Then came the fire's hungry gaze.
It licked the walls, it kissed the air,
It left us nothing—just despair.

Barefoot souls on frozen ground,
Watching as our past burned down.
Yet in the ruin, we still stand—
Holding on with trembling hands.

What Flames Cannot Take

Flames can steal the roof, the walls,
The frames that lined the shadowed halls.
They turn to dust the things we own,
Leave only ruins made of stone.

Yet love is not a thing of wood,
Not bricks, nor glass, nor beams that stood.
What fire takes, it cannot claim,
The heart still beats beyond the flame.

Words Unspoken

I shape my thoughts like fragile glass,
Afraid they'll shatter if they pass.
They sit behind my tightened lips,
A message lost in fingertips.

I want to speak, to let them go,
But silence is the voice I know.
Yet in my eyes, in every glance,
I beg the world to understand.

Stuck Between Syllables

My thoughts run fast, my tongue stands still,
A battle fought against my will.
Each sound a step, a fragile climb,
But some collapse before their time.

They wait, they watch, their eyes so wide,
I fight to speak, to stand with pride.
But though my words may twist and break,
They're mine to own, my voice to take.

When We Were Words

We were pages filled with ink,
Stories deeper than we'd think.
Every word a tethered thread,
A map we wove, a path we said.

But now the lines have come undone,
Your voice is gone, the tale is run.
And all that's left are echoes spun,
Of words we whispered, now as one.

A Voice That Shakes

A voice that shakes is still a voice,
Not silence bound, but caught by choice.
For words are rivers, wild and free,
And though they tremble, they still speak me.

So do not rush, do not pretend,
That pauses mark a story's end.
For even broken words take flight,
And turn to stars in silent night.

Static on the Line

I dial your number, hear the tone,
But silence tells me you're not home.
The static hums, the distance grows,
A voice now lost in dial tones.

If words could cross the space we share,
Would you still like to listen? Would you care?
Or are we echoes, lost, unsaid,
Two voices speaking to the dead?

Ghost of Who I Was

I see my face in shattered glass,
A stranger's eyes, a haunted past.
I used to laugh, I used to dream,
Now all I do is chase the need.

I hear my mother call my name,
But shame won't let me look her way.
She prays for me—I wish she knew,
I pray for me, I'm praying too.

Too Much, Too Loud, Too Fast

My mind's a room with no escape,
Clocks that tick but won't keep pace.
A flood of thoughts, a tangled thread,
A war that rages in my head.

The world expects, demands, assumes,
But I am lost inside this room.
I try to speak, to scream, to cry,
But all that leaves me is a sigh.

The Room is Shrinking

The walls move closer, inch by inch,
The air is tight, my chest is clenched.
A hundred things, a thousand more,
Yet all I want is out the door.

But even air feels hard to find,
Trapped inside my crowded mind.
I need the sky, the stars, the sea,
To stretch beyond what's suffocating me.

A Flood With No Rain

The storm is here, but skies are clear,
A drowning wave inside my ear.
No one sees, no one knows,
How deep can this unseen river flow?

I tread the waters, fight the tide,
But it pulls stronger from inside.
If only I could swim to shore,
If only I could take no more.

A Love That Burns

You loved me like the sun loves earth,
Just close enough to prove my worth.
But if I strayed too near the light,
You turned your warmth to endless night.

I fed the fire, I tried, I bled,
Yet still, you let the embers spread.
Until I stood in flames so high,
That love became my last goodbye.

Puppeteer

Strings wrapped tight around my bones,
A voice not mine, yet still my own.
You pulled, you shaped, you made me dance,
A marionette of circumstance.

Yet strings can snap, and ties can break,
And even dolls can feel the ache.
So now I stand, with hands set free,
No longer yours, but only me.

Overthinking

I replay the words, I rewind the scene,
A movie looping inside of me.
Every sentence, every glance,
Every silence—was it chance?

I dissect it all, piece by piece,
Yet find no answers, no release.
Just spinning my wheels, just sleepless nights,
An anxious mind in endless flight.

The Invisible Battle

No scars to show, no wounds to see,
Yet still, this war rages in me.
A battle fought with every breath,
A quiet war that feels like death.

I stand, I smile, I play the part,
Yet carry panic in my heart.
And though I wish to set it free,
It fights, it stays—it conquers me.

I Write These Poems

I write these poems to set things free,
The thoughts that claw inside of me.
The words unspoken, trapped too tight,
Now spill like ink into the night.

I write these poems for the ache,
For love that stayed, for hearts that break.
For silent wars, for restless minds,
For all the things we leave behind.

I write these poems for the lost,
For every dream that paid a cost.
For those who scream but make no sound,
For those still searching to be found.

I write these poems so I don't drown,
To pull the darkness, lay it down.
To shape the chaos into art,
And bleed my soul through every part.

I write these poems to feel, to breathe,
To leave a mark, to let you see.
And if my words can reach just one,
Then maybe healing has begun.

Sunlight in Slow Motion

The sky unfolds, a painter's dream,
Brushstrokes melting into streams.
Amber, crimson, gold ignite,
Chasing ghosts away with light.

The world still wakes, the air is thin,
A hush before the day begins.
And in this moment, soft and bright,
The past dissolves into the light.

After the Storm

The rain had drowned the world last night,
Left echoes thick, left hearts too tight.
But here it comes, the light still grows,
A sunrise soft as fallen snow.

The sky, reborn in hues of grace,
A quiet hand upon my face.
And though the storm still haunts my mind,
The dawn reminds me: hope is kind.

First Light

Before the world has woken up,
Before your coffee fills the cup,
Before the rush, before the sound,
The sunrise lays upon the ground.

It stretches long, it takes its time,
A steady hand, a perfect rhyme.
And in the hush of golden beams,
We find ourselves inside a dream.

Ink Runs Dry

I've poured my soul in lines of ink,
Let every thought spill out and sink.
But now the words just feel too thin,
A hollow echo deep within.

I write and write, yet nothing stays,
Just empty lines and endless days.
Perhaps it's time to close the page,
To walk away, to turn the page.

Unfinished

Not every poem needs an end,
Not every thought needs ink to mend.
Some things are best left incomplete,
Some words too raw, some wounds too deep.

So here I stop, mid-line, mid-thought,
A story left, a lesson taught.
For even silence has its place,
A pause, a breath, a needed space.

Letting Go of the Words

I have written through the night,
Fought my demons, won the fight.
But now my hands begin to shake,
My mind has had all it can take.

The words will wait, the ink can rest,
I've given all, I've done my best.
So here I stop, no grand goodbyes—
Just quiet hands and tired eyes.

Almost Touching

I stretch my hands, I beg, I plead,
For something I will never see.
A love that fades before it stays,
A dream dissolved in morning haze.

It lingers close, it breathes my air,
It whispers soft, it strokes my hair.
Yet when I turn, it slips away,
A phantom that was never mine to claim

The Language of Colors

Blue speaks softly, calm and deep,
A lullaby the oceans keep.
Red ignites with burning light,
A fire that roars into the night.

Yellow hums like laughter free,
A sunbeam dancing wild and free.
Green is quiet, steady, strong,
The color where the earth belongs.

And yet, in shades where colors blend,
A story shifts, begins, extends.
For every hue, a voice, a place,
A silent song in time and space.

The Hands That Raised Me

Calloused fingers, tired eyes,
Hands that lifted, hands that tried.
They held me firm, they shaped my way,
Yet asked for nothing, not a pay.

And now I see what time has done,
Their hands now weaker, worn by sun.
I take them now, as they once did,
And hold the love that never hid.

The House We Grew In

The walls still hum with echoes past,
Footsteps, laughter—built to last.
A home of voices, hands, and names,
Yet time has played its quiet games.

We've drifted far, like autumn leaves,
Yet something deeper never leaves.
For even walls that crack and break,
Hold love that time cannot erase.

Glitter in the Air

Life is like glitter—floating, fading,
Beautiful for a moment, then gone.
You try to hold it,
But it slips through your fingers,
Leaving only specks behind.

We chase the shine,
Thinking it will last,
But even the brightest things
Can disappear in the wind.

What Glitter Leaves Behind

Not all glitter stays in sight.
Some of it sticks,
Some washes away,
Some gets lost in places you never check.

The words we say,
The love we give,
The moments we don't realize matter—
They are the glitter left behind
When we're gone.

Glitter is Not Gold

They told me life should sparkle,
That happiness shines,
That success glows.
But glitter doesn't mean gold.

Sometimes, the shiniest things
Are empty inside.
And the real things—the strong things—
Aren't the ones that catch the light.

Drowned in White

Snow falls heavy, burying the world,
layer by layer, it takes everything.
No sound, no color, just the weight of winter
pressing down like a forgotten memory.

Steps disappear as fast as they come,
voices swallowed before they can reach.
Nothing moves, nothing speaks,
only the wind, whispering things I can't understand.

Somewhere under all this, the earth still breathes,
waiting for the thaw, waiting to be seen.
But for now, everything is lost,
drowned in white.

Deep Snow, Quiet Earth

The snow is deep enough to hide anything.
Footprints, mistakes, even time.
It settles into the cracks,
fills the spaces where warmth used to live.

Trees bend under the weight,
silent, still, waiting.
The air is thick with cold,
thick with something heavier than silence.

I stand in the middle of it all,
watching the world disappear.
And I wonder—
if I stayed long enough,
would I disappear too?

Buried

Snow keeps falling.
Soft at first, then relentless.
It covers roads, rooftops,
the past, the present, everything.

Somewhere under it all,
grass is frozen, rivers are waiting,
but you wouldn't know it.
Not now.

Not when the world is buried,
not when the sky keeps falling.
Not when everything feels so far away.

Winter's Weight

The sky sinks lower, heavy with snow,
pressing the world into silence.
Everything softens, everything slows,
buried beneath the hush of white.

The trees stand like frozen statues,
their limbs bowed under the weight of waiting.
Roads disappear, swallowed whole,
as if the world has finally given up its shape.

Inside, the warmth hums low and steady,
a fragile flicker against the deep cold.
But outside, winter stretches wide,
holding its breath, holding time still,
refusing to let go.

Spring's Ghosts

The first thaw comes not with flowers,
but with water slipping through the cracks,
slowly unraveling winter's grip.
Ice melts into puddles,
snow shrinks into memory,
but the ghosts of frost still linger.

The trees remember their losses,
the way the cold stripped them bare.
Their branches, twisted and raw,
reach out for the sun,
but they do not bloom yet.

Beneath the soil, the roots wait,
listening for the whisper of warmth.
And then, slowly, softly,
the earth exhales.

Summer's Breath

Heat rises from the pavement,
shimmering like something alive.
The air is thick with cicada songs,
with sweat and gasoline and sunburnt skin.

The days stretch long, lazy and golden,
as if time itself has slowed down,
drifting in waves of dust and heat.
Somewhere, laughter rolls like thunder,
carefree and endless,
as if summer could last forever.

But the sky holds its secrets,
storms gathering beyond the horizon,
a reminder that even the sun
must someday rest.

Autumn's Exit

Leaves let go without resistance,
floating to the ground
like forgotten words.

The air carries the scent of endings—
smoke curling from chimneys,
earth damp with rain,
the last trace of warmth
fading from the wind.

The trees don't fight it.
They know when it's time to rest.
They stand tall as they shed their past,
knowing spring will bring them new skin.

But for now, they are bare,
standing against the cold,
unafraid of what's to come.

The First Storm

It begins as a whisper,
a distant murmur in the sky.
The wind shifts, uneasy,
twisting through the trees
like something searching for a home.

Then, the sky unravels.
Thunder cracks, splitting the silence.
Lightning claws at the dark,
a flicker of rage before the rain falls—
slow at first, then all at once.

The trees bow, the rooftops tremble.
Some things will stand,
some things will break.
And in the morning,
the world will be different.

The Flood

Water moves slow at first,
seeping through cracks,
soaking the edges of things,
like a warning nobody listens to.

Then, it comes all at once—
rivers overflowing, streets vanishing,
houses standing ankle-deep in memory.
It does not ask permission.
It does not care what it takes.

When it's gone,
it leaves behind silence,
muddy footprints of the past,
and people staring at what remains,
wondering how to start again.

The Blizzard

Snow does not fall gently tonight.
It comes in waves, sharp and endless,
erasing roads, swallowing fences,
turning the world into a shapeless blur.

The wind howls, pushing against doors,
rattling windows, sneaking into cracks.
It whispers in voices we cannot understand,
ancient and unrelenting.

By morning, the world is buried.
The sky is quiet again,
as if nothing ever happened.
But beneath the snow,
the earth still remembers.

Midnight Rain

The storm does not come with thunder,
no warning, no wild wind.
It comes soft, secret,
falling against windows,
pooling in the quiet corners of the night.

It hums on rooftops,
melts into the earth,
whispering things only the darkness can hear.
By morning, it is gone,
but the air still carries its weight,
the soil still drinks its memory.

And somewhere, beneath the damp leaves,
something small begins to grow.

The Last Leaf

One leaf clings to the branch,
trembling in the wind.
It is the last one, the last memory,
a small defiance against the cold.

It should have let go with the others,
but something inside it still holds on—
not out of strength,
not out of fear,
but because it is not ready.

The wind pulls harder,
the sky grows colder,
and finally, finally,
it lets go.

And in that moment,
there is nothing left but silence,
and the promise of spring.

Liminality

It's the space between—
not where you were,
not where you're going,
just here.

A waiting room with no doors,
a bridge with no end in sight.
The past is close enough to touch,
but it won't take you back.
The future waits,
but it won't reach for you yet.

So you stand in the middle,
not lost, not found,
just stuck.

No map, no signs,
just time stretching too long,
just the weight of change pressing in.

You're not who you were.
You're not who you'll be.
You're just here—
in between,
and that has to be enough.

Home

It took me years to learn
that home isn't a place.
Not a house, not a town,
not the rooms I used to know.

Home is the people who stay,
the ones who make the world feel softer.
The ones who see you,
even when you don't see yourself.

I've lost houses.
I've left cities.
But home has always found me
in the ones who love me
Anyway.

Becoming

I used to think growing up
meant having answers.
Now I know it's mostly
learning how to live with questions.

Who am I?
What do I want?
Where am I going?

Some days, I think I know.
Other days, I feel like a stranger
to my own reflection.

But maybe that's the point—
to keep moving,
to keep becoming,
even when you don't know
what comes next.

Late Nights and Long Thoughts

Some nights stretch longer than they should,
filled with memories I didn't invite.
Conversations I should have had,
people I should have kept,
mistakes that still whisper my name.

The past is quiet but never gone.
It sits in the corner, waiting,
reminding me that time moves forward,
but some things never really leave.

The Things I Don't Say

There are words I hold in my throat,
too heavy to speak,
too loud to let go.

I carry them through conversations,
smiling, nodding,
pretending they don't press against my ribs.

Maybe one day,
I'll open my mouth,
and they'll come out like breath—
soft, easy, finally free.

But not today.

The Person I Used to Be

I walk past old places,
see shadows of myself in the glass.
A younger version, standing there,
full of ideas, full of dreams
that don't quite fit anymore.

I wonder if they'd recognize me now,
if they'd ask what happened.
If they'd be proud.
Or if they'd just walk by,
thinking I was someone else.

Copyright © [2025] by Makayla Anderson
All rights reserved. No part of this book may be reproduced, stored in a retrieval system, or transmitted in any form or by any means—electronic, mechanical, photocopying, recording, or otherwise—without prior written permission from the author, except for brief quotations in reviews or articles.